NIGHT GOLF

by WILLIAM MILLER

illustrated by

CEDRIC LUCAS

LEE AND LOW Inc.   New York

For my father, who played the game so well—W.M.

*To my family and those who had the courage
to be and think different—C.L.*

LEE & LOW BOOKS, Inc., 95 Madison Avenue, New York, NY 10016

Printed in Hong Kong by South China Printing Co. (1988) Ltd.

Book Design by Christy Hale
Book Production by The Kids at Our House

The text is set in Charlotte Book
The illustrations are rendered in pastel and colored pencil

10   9   8   7   6   5   4   3   2
First Edition

Library of Congress Cataloging-in-Publication Data
Miller, William
Night golf/by William Miller; illustrated by Cedric Lucas.—1st ed.
p.   cm.
Summary: Despite being told that only whites can play golf, James becomes a caddy and is
befriended by an older African American man who teaches him to play on the course at night.
ISBN 1-880000-79-2
1. Afro-Americans—Juvenile fiction.   [1. Afro-Americans—Fiction.   2. Golf—Fiction.
3. Prejudices—Fiction.]   I. Lucas, Cedric, ill.   II. Title.
PZ7.M63915Ni   1999
[E]—dc21   98-47168
                                                                       CIP   AC

AUTHOR'S NOTE

NOT LONG AGO, professional golf could only be played by white golfers. In fact, throughout most of this century, African Americans were denied the right to play at many private and even public golf courses. The closest most could come to playing golf was to serve as a caddie, carrying heavy bags for others.

In some places, a few ingenious African American caddies found a way to swing a club on the green—at night. Under a cloak of darkness, they perfected their skills by striking the ball in the moonlight. A few even excelled at the game, including Charlie Sifford. The former caddie became the first African American admitted to the PGA tour in 1962.

More than a decade later, in 1975, Lee Elder, another former caddie, became the first African American to play in the prestigious Masters Tournament.

In 1997, Tiger Woods, whose father is African American and whose mother is Asian American, won the Masters Tournament by the largest stroke margin in its history.

JAMES LOVED SPORTS.
More than anything he wanted
to be an athlete, prove he could
play something well. But James
was too short for basketball, too
small to carry a pigskin across
the goal line....

One morning, he found a golf
bag in a garbage can. Inside was
a single, rusted club, a pack of
old balls.

In the field behind his house,
James hit shot after shot. At first
he couldn't control the club or
the flight of the ball. But the
more he practiced, the easier it
became to land the ball where
he wanted.

The sun was almost down when his father called to him from the back porch. "I'm late for the loading dock, son. You better get inside now."

"Wait, Dad. I found this old club and I want to show you…."

"That's real nice, James," his father said sadly. "But I wouldn't get my heart set on playing golf. There's no room for a black man in that game."

James didn't understand. All he knew was how good the club felt in his hand, how natural it was to strike the ball.

The next day, James took the streetcar to the only golf course in town. There, staring through the fence, he saw what his father was talking about. The golfers were all white men dressed in funny clothes. The only blacks were the men who walked beside them, carrying their bags.

"Can I help you, boy?" A white man with a clipboard stood beside him.

"I want, I want...." James was so nervous he almost turned and ran.

"You must be here about the dishwasher's job. You need to see the dining hall manager. Go around back, like you're supposed to."

James almost did what the man told him. All of his life, he had been doing what white men told him to do. But this time was different.

"I want to carry a bag," James said. "Like those guys. That's the job I came here for."

The man looked at him closely. "Well, we are short a boy or two. But being a caddy's no easy job—especially for a kid. You've got to keep quiet unless one of the members asks you for something. No one likes a smart-mouthed caddy."

"I'll do whatever it takes," James said. "I really want to play—I mean caddy."

The man laughed out loud. "For a second, I thought you said you wanted to play golf. Heck, boy. This is a game for white folks only—rich white folks at that."

James spent the rest of the morning waiting for his first round as a caddy. At last a tall man walked up to him, carrying two sets of clubs.

"I'm Charlie," he said with a slow smile. "I've been a caddy for twenty years now. I hear you want to be one, too."

James didn't get a chance to speak. Charlie loaded a heavy bag on his back, then walked off towards the first tee.

Two men dressed in green sweaters were waiting for them. Charlie handed one man a driver, and James did the same.

"Son, I've got ten drivers and can't hit one of them. Give me a three wood or go on home." Both golfers laughed, and Charlie laughed too. James felt like a fool.

Neither man played very well. They spent more time cursing than lining up their shots. James spent most of the round looking for lost balls in the pine needles and underbrush. Charlie watched him out of the corner of his eye, and, once, he even winked.

But as the sun climbed higher into the sky, James began to notice how the course was laid out. He memorized sand bunkers and water hazards. He played the golfers' shots over in his mind.

James knew that golf was his game, and he wanted to prove it by playing. What difference did the color of his skin make?

"Think you still want to be a caddy?" Charlie pulled a bottled soda from the cooler. The round was over, and James was covered with sweat. His head ached from standing in the sun so long.

"I never wanted to be a caddy," James said, too tired to care who heard him. "I wanted—I want to play golf, not watch other people play it."

Charlie chuckled softly. "You remind me of someone else. You remind me of a kid who came out here a long time ago. He was a farm boy who hated to plow. His folks moved to town, and his daddy helped build this golf course. He wanted to play golf just like you—so bad he could taste it."

"What happened to him?" James asked.

"You're looking at him," Charlie said with a sad smile.

James felt sick inside. He felt sorry for the older man, but he also felt sorry for himself. Would he still be a caddy in twenty years?

"You never get to play, do you?" James asked Charlie.

"I never said that, did I?" He had a funny look in his eye. "No sir, I never did say that."

"Where do you play, then? Out in a field, a pasture, where?"

"Pastures are for cows, my boy. I play right here, on this beautiful golf course." Charlie winked at him for the second time that day.

James was really confused. Everyone was teasing him, making him feel like a silly kid. "I'm going home now," he said. "I've had enough of this place!"

"Too bad," Charlie said. "I plan on getting in nine holes myself." Then he leaned forward and whispered in James's ear. "You come back tonight, when the moon is up. I'll leave the side gate open for you."

James was sure Charlie was joking, that somehow a trick was being played on him. But he came back that night—he just couldn't stay away.

The clubhouse and the course were dark. The only light was the moon slowly climbing the night sky. James felt like a thief, but the side gate was open, just like Charlie said it would be.

"Are you lost or something?" A deep voice asked from the shadows. James almost ran, ready to give up golf if it kept him out of jail.

Charlie stepped into the moonlight, a set of clubs slung over his shoulder. "It's time to play golf," he said proudly, "not watch it."

Charlie teed up on the first hole. Before James had time to say a word, Charlie struck the ball down the dark fairway.

Together, they walked through the shadows. James heard an owl's weird cry, saw what might have been a rabbit run across their path.

"What's that?" Charlie asked, pointing to the ground.

"I don't see a thing," James said, telling the truth.

"Look closely, son, if you want to learn this game," Charlie insisted.

James stared at the dark ground, the faint moonlight helping him see the outline of a small rock. Charlie pulled a club from his bag and swung smoothly in the moonlight. The rock was a ball, and James saw it glitter before it fell on the far-off green.

"How'd you do that?" James asked. "How'd you know where the ball landed the first time? Can you see in the dark or something? Tell me—"

"Hold on, now. You've got a lot to learn, and I plan on teaching you everything."

And Charlie taught him well. For the rest of the summer, James came back to the course, the moonlight, to the strangest game of golf ever played. He learned to play by feel, to shut out everything except the club and the ball.

But when the sun came up, James was still a caddy. His skin was still the wrong color. He would never play golf in the daylight. Or so it seemed....

One morning, James stood on the first tee. Once more, he and Charlie were caddying for two men who couldn't hit the ball, even in the bright sunshine. Dr. Jones and his partner, Mr. Phelps, had the best equipment and all the time to play in the world. They had everything, James thought, everything but skill.

When Dr. Jones sliced his drive into the woods, James muttered under his breath, "I can do better than that."

"What did you say, son?" Dr. Jones asked.

"Nothing, sir. I didn't say anything," James replied without looking up.

"This boy doesn't know the rules, Charlie," Mr. Phelps said, pointing at James. "Caddies are supposed to know their place. They're supposed to keep quiet."

"I'm not his daddy," Charlie said quietly.

Dr. Jones was turning red. "Okay, son. Let's see how good you are. It's one thing to say you can do something—another thing to prove it." He put the driver in James's hand. "Go on, show us."

Everyone was looking at James. The golfers behind them, even the men on the next fairway had stopped to watch. His palms were sweating as he teed up the ball. What if he hooked it? What if he sliced it?

Then James remembered the day he found the club in the garbage can. He remembered how good he felt each time he struck the ball that first day, and every time since, in the summer moonlight. There was nothing like that feeling in the whole world. That freedom....

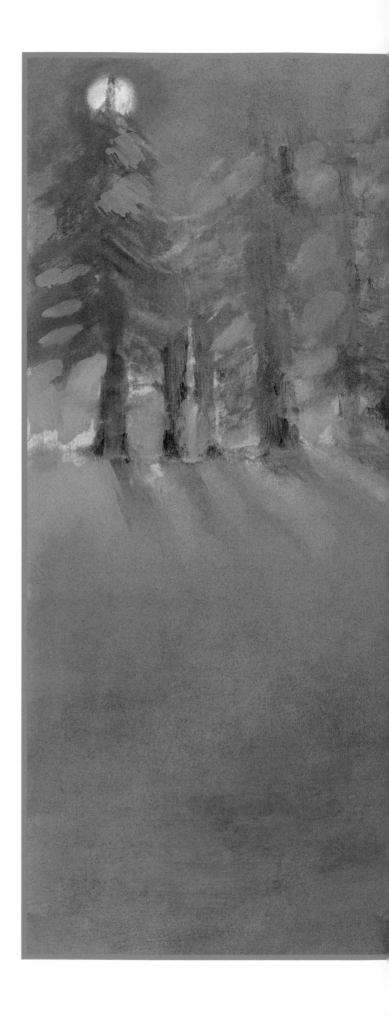

He could be a caddy for the rest of his life or prove himself now.

"Steady, James," Charlie said from behind him. "Just remember what I taught you, what we learned together."

James closed his eyes and saw the fairway in his mind. The moon was rising slowly above the tall pine trees. The night air was cool on his face….

He drew the club behind his back and swung cleanly through the ball.

"Did you see that?" Dr. Jones shouted. "He almost drove the green with his eyes closed!"

"Do it again, son," Mr. Phelps said nervously. "I think you just got lucky."

But it wasn't luck that drove the ball down the middle of the fairway, over and over again.

A crowd soon gathered around the tee. "Teach me to do that," someone shouted. "If you can teach me to hit like that, I'll carry your bag," another man said. The crowd followed them off the tee, from one hole to the next.

"Don't get a big head, now," Charlie whispered as they
walked ahead of the crowd. "You've still got a lot to learn."

"Will you teach me?" James asked.

"That's a promise, son," Charlie said with a wink.

AFRICAN AMERICANS IN GOLF: IN BRIEF

1899

Dr. George F. Grant, an African American dentist in Boston, designs and patents the first golf tee.

1926

United Golf Association (UGA) is formed to create a professional league for African American golfers. Its first tournament takes place at an all-African American country club in Stow, Massachusetts. Known as the "peanut circuit," the UGA offered little prize money and virtually no publicity.

1940s

African American professional golfers, along with champion boxer and golf enthusiast Joe Louis, fight against the Professional Golf Association's "Caucasian clause," which states that membership is only open to "professional golfers of the Caucasian Race." In 1946, Louis hosts his own tournament, the Joe Louis Open.

1948

Two of UGA's best golfers, Teddy Rhodes and Bill Spiller, win an out-of-court settlement to gain entrance to Professional Golf Association (PGA) "open" tournaments. In response, the PGA changes its tournaments from being open to "invitationals," with more restrictions to exclude people of color.

late 1950s

The NAACP keeps public golf courses open by taking cases to the Supreme Court, while Southern cities try to get around desegregation laws by leasing out municipal golf courses to private firms that can keep out black members.

1960s

In November, 1961, golf becomes the last major sport to be officially integrated. The PGA strikes its "Caucasian clause" from its constitution after threat of legal action by California's Attorney General, Stanley Mosk. Mosk became a crusader after a chance meeting on a golf course with Charlie Sifford, an African American golf pioneer. Sifford would become the first African American golfer to win the Hartford Open (1967) and the Los Angeles Open (1969). Meanwhile, the introduction of golf carts replaced the caddy system that had provided many African Americans access onto the course.

1975

Lee Elder becomes the first African American to play the Masters Tournament. Earlier in his career, Elder nearly upset Jack Nicklaus in a sudden death playoff on a nationally televised tournament in 1968.

1997

Tiger Woods becomes the youngest champion and first African American to win The Masters in Augusta, Georgia.

Source:

Altman, Linda. *Lee Elder: The Daring Dream*. St. Paul, MN: EMC Corporation, 1976.

Gullo, Jim. "Par for the Course," *American Legacy*, Fall 1997.

Sifford, Charlie with Jim Gullo. *Just Let Me Play: The Story of Charlie Sifford, the First Black PGA Golfer*. Latham, New York: British American Publishing, 1992.